Written By
Douglas G. Russell
Edited by John C. Traynor

Printed and   Published by

INGLIS ALLEN

© 1995 Inglis Allen.
All Rights Reserved
ISBN 0 9519694 8 X
£5.25

1996

CONTENTS

Prince of Players

Brian Laudrup

AUGUST, and the beginning of a new season, is traditionally one of the more relaxed months in Scottish Football.

As was customary, many Rangers fans hoped that this campaign would include early away visits to either Easter Road or Tynecastle in Edinburgh (so that they could attend an event at the Capital's prestigious Arts Festival after the game, of course).

It would not have been the first time that the merits of a radical production of Shakespeare's 'Hamlet' were discussed after such a visit to the East! But it would be another 'Prince of Denmark' who would be the sole topic of conversation throughout Ibrox Stadium at final whistle time today. Brian Laudrup was about to explode onto the Scottish Football scene.

There was definitely something in the air that afternoon, although this first game of Season 1994/95 against Motherwell at Ibrox was typical in many ways.

Just before kick-off, Chairman David Murray once again unfurled the Championship flag to begin proceedings. Expectations remained high for the coming campaign despite the European set-back in Athens three days earlier.

PRINCE OF PLAYERS

A Mark Hateley headed goal had been cancelled out by Motherwell's equaliser and it looked as if the points would be shared, with the score still 1-1 and the second half slipping away. To be fair, Alex McLeish's team had played well and probably deserved to take something from the game.

Enter 'The Prince', stage right.

A quite magnificent mazy run from just outside the Rangers penalty area left defenders trailing as Laudrup bore down on the Motherwell goal. The Dane released his pass just at the right time into the path of Duncan Ferguson (gone but not forgotten!) for the big striker to score a memorable goal.

It was probably then that the Ibrox masses realised for the first time just how talented a player Walter Smith had brought to the club.

This was just the beginning, however, as a whole series of sparkling virtuoso displays were to follow and thus grace the quest for that 'Magnificent Seven' of Championships all-in-a-row.

Without a doubt, 'Player of the Year'. Maybe even 'Player of the Decade'.

Overleaf: (Top Left) Laudrup scores against Falkirk in a 2-0 victory at Brockville.

(Bottom Left) Brian in midfield control against Aberdeen at Pittodrie.

(Top Right) 'Godrup' in full flight at Easter Road against Hibernian.

(Bottom Right) 'Prince of Players'.

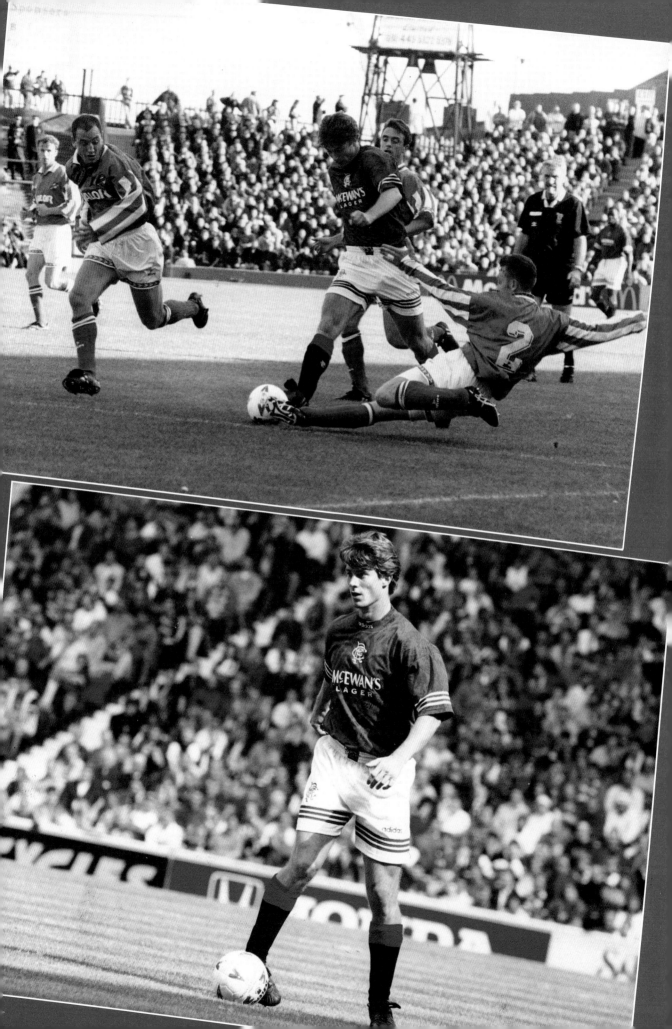

BLUE BLADE

CHARLIE MILLER

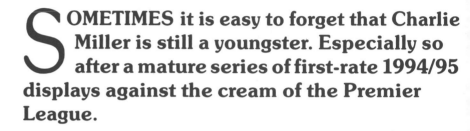

SOMETIMES **it is easy to forget that Charlie Miller is still a youngster. Especially so after a mature series of first-rate 1994/95 displays against the cream of the Premier League.**

The Ibrox faithful will recall with relish that marvellous moment, now captured in time, when Charlie 'stole' the ball from Celtic's Boyd to set up Mark Hateley's opening strike in the 3-1 'Hampden Happening'.

Just the thought of it still manages to produce a wry smile.

Remember, too, some important goals in the period, not least of which was his first-minute effort against Hearts at Ibrox in January 1995 which proved to be the ultimate winner.

It is a fact of football life that many so-called 'Superkids' burst onto the scene and just as quickly disappear with every passing season.

In this case, however, there is a school of thought that here, indeed, is a young player with the genuine potential to go all the way.

STRAIGHT TO THE TOP!

'94 Celebrations '95

Stuart McCall celebrates his last minute winner in the 3-2 victory over Falkirk at Brockville, January 1995.

Opposite: (Top) It's a 'Pyramid of Joy' at Ibrox as Basile Boli is hoisted aloft by Mark Hateley, assisted by McCall. (Bottom) Craig Moore leads the celebrations after his strike in the 2-2 Pittodrie draw against Aberdeen.

Bluebells are Blue

Premier League, 30th October 1994

CELTIC 1   **RANGERS 3**

Hateley (25, 42 mins)
Laudrup (65 mins)

HOLLYWOOD comes to Hampden. This was the day that the truly improbable happened but that would be later. . . .

The scene had been set for a 'Battle Royal' between the League Cup finalists and the reigning Champions. Celtic naturally approached the game on a high after having disposed of Aberdeen earlier that week in the semi-final of the 'Coca-Cola Cup' at Ibrox, whereas Rangers' previous outing had resulted in a 2-1 defeat at Fir Park against Championship challengers, Motherwell.

This was the 234th league meeting between the clubs, with Rangers having won on 91 occasions, Celtic 73 and the remaining 69 drawn.

Although Rangers had only been allocated 4,000 spaces in the sell-out crowd of 34,000, that resolute band of followers could clearly be heard as Stuart McCall (Captain for the day in the absence through injury of Richard Gough) led out the Rangers team. Alan McLaren was making his first appearance in a Rangers strip, having completed the transfer from Hearts which took Dave McPherson back to Tynecastle as part of the deal. His was to be an immense contribution to the Ibrox cause that day.

BLUEBELLS ARE BLUE

Rangers began in dominant fashion with a Hateley netbound header being cleared off the line in the first minute. Shortly afterwards, the 'Light Blues' were denied a stonewall penalty when Hateley was brought crashing down to the ground by Barry Smith – but the striker would not be denied for long . . . . .

In 25 minutes, Rangers deservedly went ahead as the 'Dark Destroyer' hit the target for one of the goals of the season. Charlie Miller dispossessed full-back Tom Boyd deep in the Celtic half and slid an inch-perfect pass into the path of the on-rushing Hateley. Although being closed down by Celtic defenders, his delightful right-foot shot from just outside the box swept past 'keeper Marshall, who remained rooted to the spot with no chance. An outstanding goal.

Although Celtic had equalised, through Byrne some fifteen minutes later, Rangers regained the lead shortly before the break, again courtesy of big Mark. The striker's second goal followed a great run and subsequent low cross by David Robertson. As before, Mark netted despite the close attention of opposition defenders. Needless to say, it was an exceptional through-ball from Brian Laudrup to the advancing Robertson that had started the move!

There may have only been 4,000 Rangers fans inside Hampden that day but theirs was the only sound to be heard as choruses of 'Bluebells Are Blue' reverberated around the National Stadium as both teams left the field at half-time.

The second period was evenly balanced, with both teams scorning opportunities to score before Rangers set the seal on an important victory with an absolute gem of a goal.

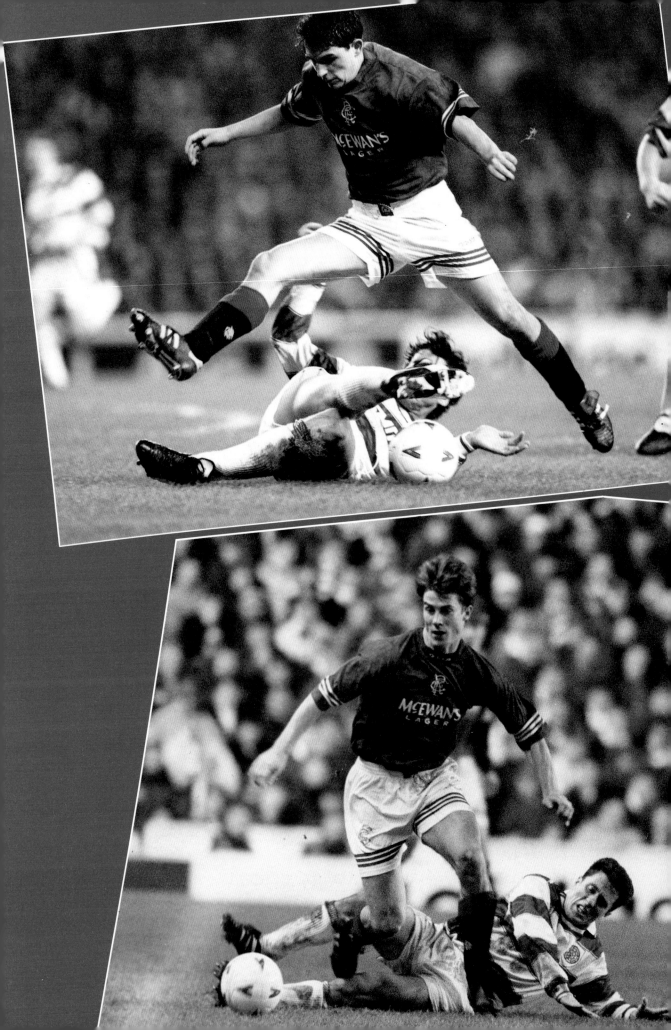

BLUEBELLS ARE BLUE

Following a long free-kick from Fraser Wishart and knock-on from that man Hateley, Brian Laudrup's electric turn of pace left defender Brian O'Neil chasing shadows in his wake as the great Dane headed for the Celtic goal and rounded Gordon Marshall to score despite a last-ditch effort from O'Neil, whose desperate lunge could not prevent the ball from hitting the back of the net.

Then we were in Hollywood as the Rangers fans became film extras from the hit movie 'Wayne's World', chanting the film's catchphrase 'We Are Not Worthy' as they bowed in unison to salute the genius of 'Godrup'. Danish Blue, indeed!

The visitors had chances to increase their lead as Celtic pushed forward, but somehow it did not really matter. The game was won and victory had been achieved with some quite considerable style.

Rangers would proceed to consolidate their position at the top of the Premier Division with six wins and two draws from the following eight games before coming face-to-face with Celtic again in early January 1995. This sequence of results included critical triumphs over both Hibernian and Motherwell, their closest rivals for the title.

A long road still had to be travelled before '7-in-a-Row' could be realised but that day's result was highly significant. Few victories throughout the campaign would taste as sweet. It had, indeed, been Something Special!

Opposite: (Above) Charlie Miller evades a despairing tackle from Brian O'Neil.
(Below) The 'Great Dane' leaves John Collins in his wake following a midfield tussle.

IBROX

Rangers staged the second Ibrox International Tournament on Saturday/Sunday, 29th/30th July 1995. Here, Ian Ferguson punches the air in delight at opening the scoring in the 4-0 rout of Steaua Bucharest, while (Opposite), 'Gazza' slots home the second, watched in the background by Stephen Wright, who had an outstanding match.

TOURNAMENT

In the final, Rangers dumped defending champions, Sampdoria, 2-0, with goals from Gordon Durie and Ally McCoist. Here, Brian Laudrup shows typical poise and control. The victorious squad (Opposite) ooze joy at wrenching the trophy from the conquerors of Tottenham Hotspur. Gordan Petric, who performed majestically, is prominent in the back row.

INTERNATIONAL

WINNERS 1995

COMBAT ZONE

Stuart McCall
'Little Big Man'

THE TENACIOUS battling qualities of Stuart McCall were required more than ever in Season 1994/95 as, week after week, the Rangers team had to be changed around mainly due to an unbelievable run of injuries to key personnel.

By early March and the latter stages of the push for '7th Heaven' glory, Stuart had become the Season's only ever-present in terms of first-team appearances. Not only that, there had been the small matter of that last-minute winning goal in the 3-2 victory over Falkirk at Brockville when the three points seemed to have disappeared.

Always willing to take responsibility in the middle of the park, the importance of his overall contribution to the cause should not be devalued.

It had been another good Season for Rangers' (and Scotland's) 'Little Big Man' of the Combat Zone.

Opposite: Stuart puts on some style in training for the next midfield mission.

IT'S ALL OVER NOW

Above: Rangers' first goal courtesy of Gordon Durie.
Opposite: Ian Durrant slots home goal No 2.

Rangers 3 Hibernian 1

Ibrox Stadium, Sunday 23rd April 1995

MAYBE it was appropriate that American legend Bob Dylan had performed at Glasgow's S.E.C. Concert Arena the previous Sunday. His catalogue of classic songs that night included 'It's All Over Now, Baby Blue'.

A little premature, maybe – but certainly it would be all over before Rangers faced Hibs for this Sunday T.V. game, as Celtic lost at Pittodrie the day before. It was now official – Rangers could not be caught and were triumphant again. Another year. . . . another Championship.

The atmosphere was predictably 'carnival' without even a lingering mathematical doubt about the destination of the Premier League title.

The game itself saw Rangers produce one of their best performances of the season in a dazzling display of sustained attacking football, creating chance after chance throughout the ninety minutes. Victory was only secured, however, in the last five minutes with quite marvellous goals from Ian Durrant and Alexei Mikhailitchenko.

The real celebrations could now begin. AT LAST!

BABY BLUE

IT'S A FACT!

Goalkeepers

BOBBY BROWN (1946-56), who always ran out onto the field of play with a new pair of white laces in his boots, only missed one league game in his first SIX seasons at Ibrox!

GEORGE NIVEN (1951-61) was the hero of the 1953 Cup Final against Aberdeen. Although he suffered a severe head injury in the first half, he re-appeared after the break, his head covered in bandages, to make a number of marvellous saves. The game was drawn – Rangers won the replay.

NORRIE MARTIN (1958-70) fractured his skull in his first match against Hearts on 23rd August 1958. Almost to the day, seven years later, on 21st August 1965, he suffered the exact same injury against Aberdeen!

PETER McCLOY (1970-86), standing 6'4" and nicknamed 'The Girvan Lighthouse' (after his birthplace in Ayrshire), was the Rangers 'keeper in the team that won the European Cup Winners' Cup in 1972, defeating Moscow Dynamo 3–2 in Barcelona.

Managers

MANY former Rangers players have gone on into management, notably in recent years:

SCOTLAND
Alex Miller (Hibernian)
Tommy McLean (Hearts)
Alex MacDonald (Airdrie)
Jimmy Nicholl (Raith Rovers)

ENGLAND
Alex Ferguson (Man. United)
Ray Wilkins (Queen's Park Rangers)
Trevor Francis (Sheffield Wednesday)

IT'S A FACT!

Trophies

RANGERS' first trophy win in five years (The League Cup Final v Celtic in 1970-71) was won by a single Derek Johnstone goal in his first 'Old Firm' match. He was still a few days short of his 17th birthday!

JOCK WALLACE became the first manager in Scottish Football to guide a team to double 'Trebles' when Rangers achieved the feat of winning the League, League Cup and Scottish Cup in Seasons 1975-76 and 1977-1978.

RANGERS won the European Cup-Winners' Cup in 1972. The Bayern Munich team they defeated in the semi-final of the competition included Beckenbauer, Müller, Maier, Roth, Breitner and Höeness. Some weeks later, all six would be in the West German national team that won the European Championship in Belgium.

Transfers

RANGERS legend Jim Baxter signed from Raith Rovers in 1960 for a then Scottish transfer record – £17,500!

WHEN Graeme Souness joined Liverpool from Middlesborough in 1978, it was for a then record fee between English clubs of £352,000.

GOALKEEPER Chris Woods was the first in a long line of 'expensive' signings by manager Graeme Souness in 1986, at a cost of £600,000 from Norwich.

TREVOR FRANCIS, who joined Rangers late in his career in 1987, was Britain's first £ million footballer.

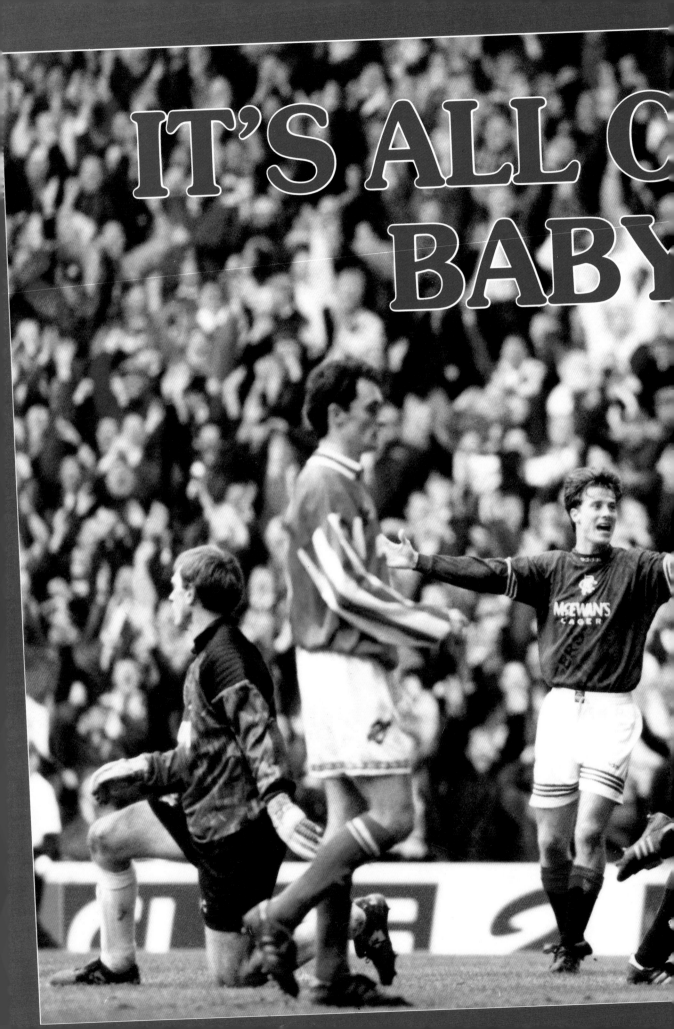

IT'S ALL O
BABY

'ER NOW
BLUE!

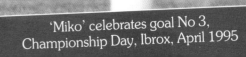

'Miko' celebrates goal No 3,
Championship Day, Ibrox, April 1995

FUN QUIZ

Season 1994/95

1. Ally McCoist's only goal of the season was in a 1-0 victory against which club?

2. On how many occasions did Rangers score four goals in the Premier League? Name the opponents.

3. Which Rangers player appeared in his first Premier League match since November 1992?

4. Who scored for Rangers in the 1995 'Ne'erday' game with Celtic at Ibrox?

5. Rangers' home attendances fell below 40,000 on only one occasion. True or False?

6. Who was top scorer in the Scottish Cup campaign?

7. Pieter Huistra's last game for Rangers was a memorable one for the player 'in more ways than one'. Why?

8. Who joined Rangers on a free transfer in August 1993 and was subsequently 'sold' on for £50,000 during 1994/95?

9. Duncan Ferguson scored against which teams before leaving for Everton?

10. Ibrox had to wait until April to witness his first goal of 1995. Name the player.

11. Which team left Ibrox unbeaten in THREE visits?

12. Name the true Ranger who reached his milestone of 250 games for the club durin' season 1994/95?

Answers on Page 46

Mr. CONSISTENT

Which Rangers player once had to be escorted by police from the Copland Road end of Ibrox (for his own safety) after being taunted by fans as he watched a game?

The honour goes to David Robertson, who had joined the Aberdeen supporters at the Coca Cola Cup semi-final v Celtic. Somehow his presence was not greatly appreciated by the fans from the 'Granite City'!

More importantly, though, his presence certainly *is* appreciated by the Rangers legions, as the speedy defender is now playing some of the best football of his career. Not only linking well with Brian Laudrup on the left side of play but scoring important goals as well.

Indeed, it was strikes from 'Robbo' that enabled Rangers to share the points in 1-1 draws with both Partick Thistle (at Firhill) and Dundee United (at Ibrox) in 1995. In the latter game, in fact, most patrons were convinced that Rangers should have been awarded *two* penalties when David himself was felled on both occasions!

Unfortunately the full back became the 11th Rangers player to undergo surgery in the course of Season 1994/95 when a metal plate (inserted years previously when with Aberdeen) had to be removed from his right foot in March.

One of the two 'penalties-that-never-were' against Dundee United, as 'Robbo' crashes to the ground in a tackle by Alex Cleland, who was later to join him at Ibrox in a surprise double-deal also involving Gary Bollan.

Mr. CONSISTENT

Few players are more resilient than 'Robbo', though. After all, his *left* foot had been broken on three separate occasions and that never kept him out for long. Nor did it diminish the power of his shot!

Sheer delight at the super strike which earned the 1-1 Ibrox draw, 4th February 1995.

It can only be a matter of time before a fully fit, injury-free David Robertson begins to amass more Scotland 'caps' and receive the international acclaim his consistency so richly deserves.

MARK-ATTACK

SOMEHOW it was inevitable. Even although Mark Hateley missed part of last season through injury (he had been an ever-present in the team until late November), Rangers' now legendary 'Hit-Man' still managed to be responsible for one of the season's greatest pleasures.

The particular game in question was Rangers' first visit to Hampden to play Celtic in a Premier League match. It became the day when the newly-refurbished National Stadium literally 'Blue-up' as Mark stunned the expectant home support into complete silence with the first of his two strikes in the first half of that engrossing encounter.

It goes without saying that Rangers naturally missed both the actual presence and, more obviously, the goalscoring abilities of such an accomplished player in the latter stages of the season.

A measure both of the man and his commitment to Rangers is that he returned to the fray (after an absence of nearly two months) in the 'all but' Championship game against Aberdeen at Ibrox on 8th April 1995 without even the benefit of a reserve outing. Almost inevitably, he scored the winner!

TIME ON HIS SIDE

Alan McLaren

IT WAS to be a very promising debut by the player tipped by many as a future captain of Rangers. Alan McLaren's first game in the blue of Ibrox following his transfer from Hearts could hardly have been more daunting – Celtic at Hampden. The pressure was ON.

Alan's contribution in defence that day was immense. He was the rock at the heart of the back four, in the absence of the *usual* steadying influence of Richard Gough, through injury.

He was to become an ever-present in the team until the end of January, during which time Rangers remained unbeaten. By his own admission, he suffered a dip in form in the latter stages of the season, but was back to his powerful best when Scotland earned a creditable point in the no-scoring draw in Moscow against European Championship hopefuls Russia, in March. Even better was to follow three days later in the form of one of the goals of the season in Rangers' significant 2-0 victory at Tannadice. A free-kick from fully 35 yards was hit with an awesome power which left Dundee United 'keeper O'Hanlon helpless.

It is easy to forget that Alan is still only in his mid-twenties, as he seems to have been competing at the highest level for so long. In years to come, Alan McLaren will surely continue to be an integral part of both the Rangers and Scotland teams. Captain of Club and Country?

TIME WILL TELL.

G.R.R.REAT GOUGH

At the start of last season, another Championship seemed a distant dream for Rangers following consecutive defeats at the hands of AEK Athens (European Cup), Celtic (Premier League) and Falkirk (Coca-Cola Cup). It was obviously going to be a long, hard slog.

In the face of just such adversity, though, traditional Rangers pride was to shine through and no-one displayed it more than Captain Richard Gough. Time and time again throughout the arduous campaign, 'Lionheart' led by example in a Rangers triumph made all the more satisfying by the fact that it was very much a transitional season at the club.

It was the courageous captaincy of Gough which inspired the team to critical victories over Dundee United, Kilmarnock, Hibernian and Motherwell during the crucial month of December in the race to eventual '7th Heaven' glory.

Just months earlier, at the end of Season 1993/94, the doubters had suggested that Richard would probably not be there when Rangers lifted the Scottish Premier Championship trophy. How wrong can you be?

Great players always rise to a challenge and Richard Gough was in no mood to become part of Rangers' past just yet. Driven by his burning desire to lead the 'Light Blues' to unsurpassed success, he proved how misguided his detractors were.

THE REST IS NOW HISTORY.

OPPOSITE: Richard scores against Hibs at Ibrox, Boxing Day 1994. Rangers won 2-0

ABOVE: Celebrating with Ian Durrant after the 'Wee Man's' penalty goal against Kilmarnock at Ibrox, February 1995, in a 3-0 win.

A Rangers Legend

Davie Cooper

SOME days have a terrible sadness about them. The tragic news that Davie Cooper had passed away on 23rd March 1995 (following a brain haemorrhage the day before) tore a hole in the hearts of thousands. And not just Rangers fans.

Signed from Clydebank for £100,000 in June 1977 by Jock Wallace, Davie's first season at Ibrox saw Rangers lift the domestic 'Treble' of League, League Cup and Scottish Cup. This was just the beginning of a glittering Ibrox career.

Many are the memories. . . . . The Drybrough Cup Final of 1979, when Davie scored his famous 'Brazilian' goal by juggling the ball past four Celtic defenders before scoring. . . . . The 1981 Scottish Cup Final replay, when he literally destroyed Dundee United in the 4-1 victory. . . . . The ferocious free-kick against Aberdeen in the 1987 Skol Cup Final that levelled the score at 1-1 and paved the way for a famous Rangers victory. Magical times indeed!

They call football 'The Beautiful Game'. . . . . well, *he* certainly played it beautifully.

First and foremost a Rangers man, Davie was, and always will be, a major part of the Club and its history. In a very special sense, he had never really left Ibrox.

DAVIE COOPER, RANGERS. Even now it's still difficult to hold back the tears.

Always
Will Be.

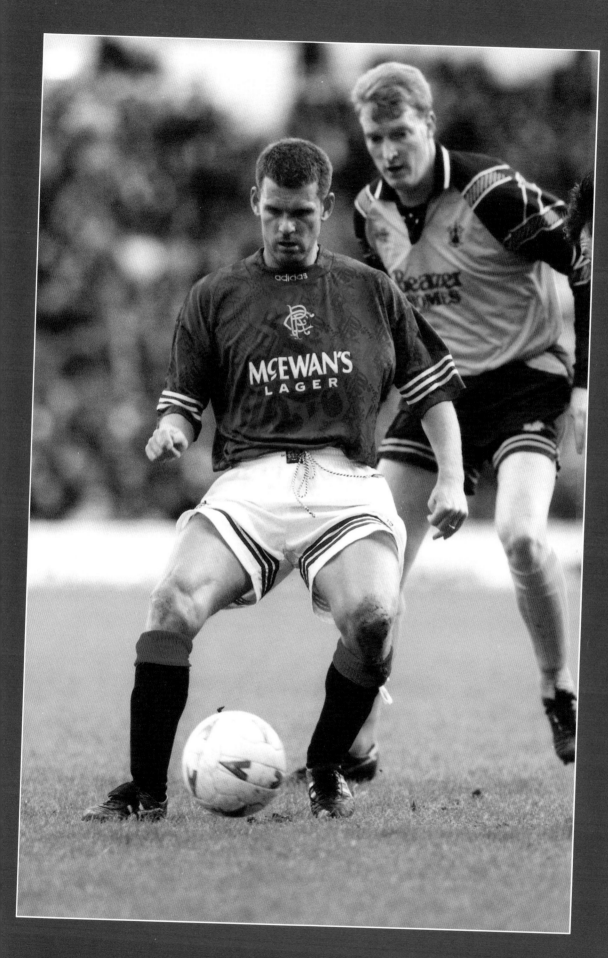

Always Will Be

Ian Durrant

IT SADDENED the heart of many a 'True Blue' when it seemed Ian Durrant's career at Ibrox was over following his 'on loan' move to Everton with Duncan Ferguson.

After all, the fans had been through so much with the 'Wee Man' during his years with Rangers. To many he was simply irreplaceable – in their eyes, 'Durranty' was, is and ALWAYS WILL BE one of them.

In the end, the proposed transfer was not confirmed and Ian returned to the Ibrox fold. His next appearance in the blue of Rangers (as substitute at home to Partick Thistle) triggered a hero's welcome – a standing ovation from the packed arena.

Goals against Dundee United at Tannadice and Kilmarnock at Ibrox (from the penalty spot) followed in comprehensive 3-0 victories for Rangers on both occasions.

Most satisfying of all, though, was his strike and 'Man of the Match' award against Aberdeen in April when the 'Light Blues' virtually clinched another Championship. His goals against the team from the 'Granite City' were *always* something special, both to the player and to the Ibrox legions.

The memories are many – but the abiding image of Ian, arms aloft in 'Victory V' celebration after scoring, is one that will remain etched in the mind. Part of Ibrox folklore, FOREVER.

FLASH
Gordon Durie

KICK OFF. Durie to Laudrup to McCall to Cleland to Boli to McLaren and back to Durie. 1-0! Simple as that – Rangers' first goal, courtesy of 'Flash Gordon'! It was April Fool's Day but *this* was no joke. A mere eleven seconds had elapsed and amazingly the Champions-Elect were already one up in the vital encounter with Dundee United at Tannadice on 1st April 1995.

Durie also played a part in Rangers' second goal, winning a free-kick some thirty-five yards out seven minutes later. He could clearly be seen urging Alan McLaren to 'have a go' prior to the centre-back blasting home a thunderbolt.

Many fans will remember Juke's fine last-minute goal against Motherwell at Fir Park on Hogmanay, when he joyfully rounded 'keeper Woods to score Rangers' third goal of the day, as well as his powerful running at the Hibs defence to create Stuart McCall's goal in the 1-1 draw at snowy Easter Road during the Scottish 'winter/spring' of early March.

It had been a difficult season for Gordon in many ways as he was regularly asked to play out of position (due to long-term injuries to both Ally McCoist and Mark Hateley) and it must be said that he coped admirably, showing great versatility.

Two seasons at the club and two League Championship medals, with the very real prospect of more to come. . . . . . and the 'Durie' isn't out on that one!

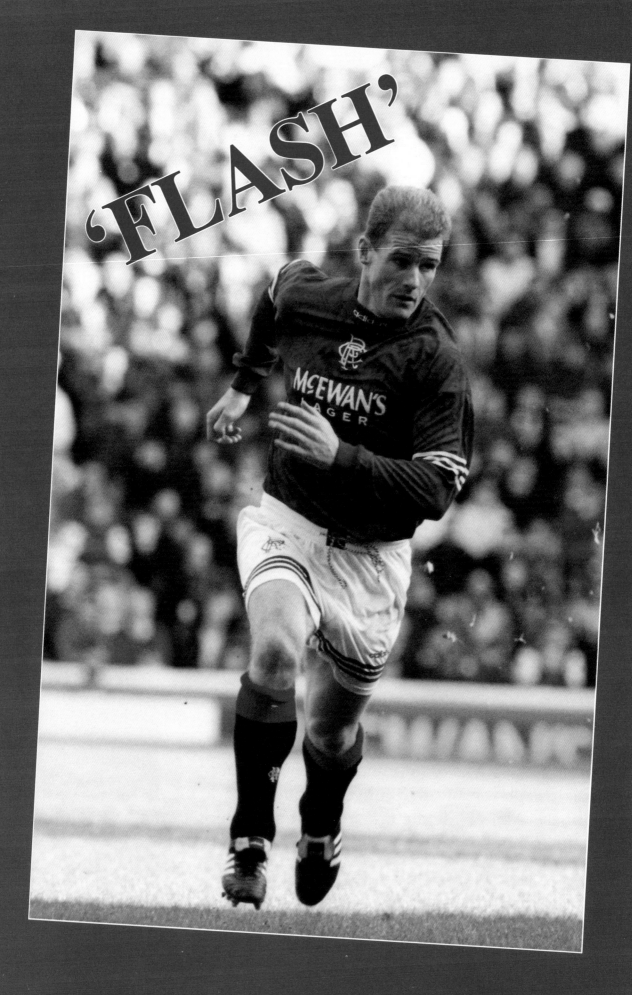

'FLASH'

FUN QUIZ ANSWERS

1. Aberdeen, Ibrox, 25.11.94.
2. None.
3. Goalkeeper Billy Thomson, against Dundee United.
4. Ian Ferguson.
5. False. They actually *never* did. (Lowest attendance was against Falkirk in the Coca-Cola Cup with a crowd of just under 40,700).
6. Brian Laudrup, with 2 goals.
7. He scored two goals in the 3-2 victory over Falkirk at Brockville (14.1.95).
8. Fraser Wishart (to Hearts).
9. Arbroath (Hat-trick' in the Coca-Cola Cup) and Motherwell (Premier League).
10. Mark Hateley.
11. Falkirk (Premier League 1-1, 2-2/Coca-Cola Cup, 2-1 victory to the 'Bairns').
12. John Brown.

ACKNOWLEDGEMENTS

Designed by Douglas Russell and John Traynor, with special assistance from Lisa Russell.

Typesetting and Origination by Inglis Allen, Kirkcaldy.

Bound in Scotland by Hunter & Foulis, Edinburgh.

All photographs supplied by *The Sun*
(*Picture Editor:* Mark Sweeney).

Photographers: Steve Welsh, Alan Ewing, Andy Barr, Peter Kelly, John Kirkby, Joe Campbell, Kenny Ramsay.

Every effort has been made by the publishers to ensure the accuracy
of all details and information in this publication.

Printed and Published in Scotland by

INGLIS ALLEN

40 Townsend Place, Kirkcaldy, Fife, Scotland KY1 1HF.
Telephone (01592) 267201   Fax (01592) 206049
ISBN 0-9519694-8-X © Inglis Allen 1995. All rights reserved.